WHO AM I?
Pre-school Workbook B

WHO AM I?
Pre-school Workbook B

Mary Jo Smith

Jerelyn Helmberger

*Educational
and
Theological Advisors*

Fr. Richard M. Hogan

Rev. John M. LeVoir

Mary Jo Smith

IMAGE OF GOD SERIES

IMAGE OF GOD, INC., BROOKLYN CENTER, MN
IGNATIUS PRESS   SAN FRANCISCO

Nihil obstat: David A. Dillon, S.T.D.
Censor Librorum

Imprimatur: + John R. Roach, D.D.
Archbishop of St. Paul and Minneapolis
August 15, 1986

Cover design and text illustrations: Barbara Harasyn

For additional information about
the Image of God program: 1–800–635–3827

Published 1994 by Ignatius Press, San Francisco
© 1986 Image of God, Inc.
All rights reserved
ISBN 0–89870–324–7
Printed in Hong Kong
Third Edition

Letter to Parents

Dear Parents,

This year your child will be using the "Who Am I?" pre-school/kindergarten program from the Image of God series. This series is centered on a new subjective emphasis found in the writings and teachings of John Paul II. This subjective turn stresses the dignity of each individual as a person made in the image of God.

The pre-school/kindergarten program has as its focus two key ideas: God and creation. These key ideas form the unifying element of the lessons. The material in each lesson revolves around fundamentals of our faith stated in terms the children can understand and remember.

You, as parents, are the primary religious educators of your children. The "Who Am I?" program has take-home materials which provide a basis for parent–child faith discussions at home. There is a set of worksheets for most lessons. Sometimes your child will bring home a completed worksheet to share. Sometimes, though, it will be up to you, as parents, to complete the worksheet with your child.

On the back of the worksheets you will find a "Note to Parents." This note contains:

a. the name and number of the lesson for easy reference, should you want to discuss a topic with your child's teacher
b. the Scripture reference for the bible story connected with the lesson (These stories themselves have been adapted to the children's ages and levels of understanding.)
c. an explanation of the main focus of the lesson, which should provide you with enough background to discuss the lesson with your child
d. the concept of faith that was the foundation of the lesson presented in question-and-answer form
e. an optional home activity for you and your child

It is hoped that through this program you and your child will grow in faith together.

Sincerely,

Lesson 1 *Directions:* Connect the dots and color the picture.

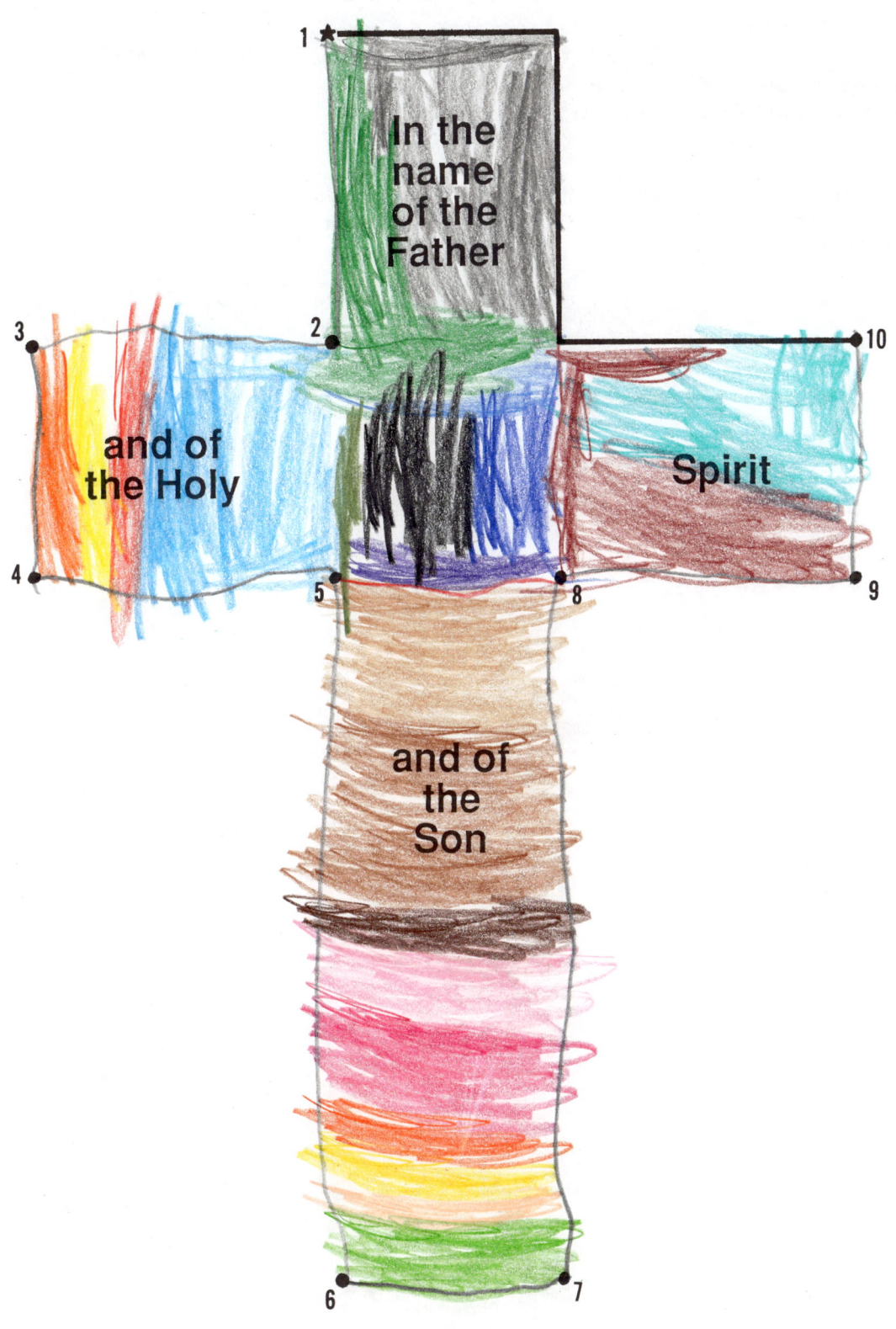

In the name of the Father
and of the Holy Spirit
and of the Son

NOTE TO PARENTS

Lesson 1: There Is One God—Trinity

In this lesson the "Sign of the Cross" and the "Glory Be" are introduced. Each time we make the "Sign of the Cross" we give praise to the three Persons of the Blessed Trinity. When we say the "Glory Be," we are showing that we believe that God always was and always will be.

Concepts of Faith

How many Gods are there?
There is one God and three Persons in the one God: Father, Son, and Holy Spirit.

What do we call the three Persons in one God?
We call the three Persons in one God the Blessed Trinity.

Activity

Review the "Sign of the Cross" and the "Glory Be" with your child: **Glory be to the Father, and to the Son, and to the Holy Spirit. As it was in the beginning is now, and ever shall be, world without end. Amen.**

Lesson 2 *Directions:* Circle the things God has made.

God made the whole world and everything in it.

55

NOTE TO PARENTS

Lesson 2: We See God in the World around Us—Creation

The story for this lesson is an adaptation of Genesis 1: 1–31. We call God Creator because He made the world and everything in it from nothing. God made all the things in the world for people to use. We can use all the things God made, but we cannot use other people. We love, praise, and thank God for the wonderful world He has given us.

Concepts of Faith

Who made the world and everything in it?
God made the world and everything in it.

Who is our Creator?
God is our Creator.

Activity

Go for a walk with your child. Point out all the wonderful things God has given us.

Lesson 2   **Creation Booklet**

God made the sun, moon, and stars.

God made the plants and trees.

56

NOTE TO PARENTS

Lesson 2: We See God in the World around Us—Creation

The story for this lesson is an adaptation of Genesis 1: 1–31. We call God Creator because He made the world and everything in it from nothing. God made all the things in the world for people to use. We can use all the things God made, but we cannot use other people. We love, praise, and thank God for the wonderful world He has given us.

Concepts of Faith

Who made the world and everything in it?
God made the world and everything in it.

Who is our Creator?
God is our Creator.

Activity

Go for a walk with your child. Point out all the wonderful things God has given us.

Lesson 2 **Creation Booklet**

God made all creatures great and small.

God made Adam and Eve in His image.

Lesson 3 *Directions:* Find and color the hidden animals.

Adam and Eve named the animals.

NOTE TO PARENTS

Lesson 3: I Am Special to God Who Made Me

The story for this lesson is an adaptation of Genesis 1:26 and Genesis 2: 18–23. We are all special because we are images of God. We can love and act the way God loves and acts. We can share God's life. As images of God, we want to teach others about God and His love for us. The good things we "think, and say, and do" help others see and learn about God through us.

Concepts of Faith

Why are we special to God?
We are special because we are made in the image of God.

Activity

Together look at pictures of your child as a baby. Discuss how much your child has grown.

Lesson 3 Directions: Circle the things animals can do.

**Animals can not act as images of God.
Only persons are made in the image of God.**

NOTE TO PARENTS

Lesson 3: I Am Special to God Who Made Me

The story for this lesson is an adaptation of Genesis 1:26 and Genesis 2: 18–23. We are all special because we are images of God. We can love and act the way God loves and acts. We can share God's life. As images of God, we want to teach others about God and His love for us. The good things we "think, and say, and do" help others see and learn about God through us.

Concepts of Faith

Why are we special to God?
We are special because we are made in the image of God.

Activity

Together look at pictures of your child as a baby. Discuss how much your child has grown.

Lesson 4   *Directions:* Connect the lines and color the picture.

THE TEN COMMANDMENTS

60

NOTE TO PARENTS

Lesson 4: Actions and Attitudes—The Ten Commandments

The story for this lesson is an adaptation of Exodus 20: 1–17. God gave us the Ten Commandments to help us know how to live as His images. They are a way of life for an image of God. The Commandments are not rules or laws forced on us, but rather the way an image of God chooses to act. When we choose to act as an image of God by following the Commandments, we show our love for God.

Concepts of Faith

How should we show our love for God?
We should show our love for God by choosing to follow the Commandments that He gave us.

Activity

Work together with your child on a small project or task. Have your child help you make a cake, wash the car, set the table, make a bed, etc. Point out the steps or directions you follow to do this project or task the correct way.

Lesson 4 *Directions:* Help Moses climb the mountain.

God gave Moses the Ten Commandments.

NOTE TO PARENTS

Lesson 4: Actions and Attitudes—The Ten Commandments

The story for this lesson is an adaptation of Exodus 20: 1–17. God gave us the Ten Commandments to help us know how to live as His images. They are a way of life for an image of God. The Commandments are not rules or laws forced on us, but rather the way an image of God chooses to act. When we choose to act as an image of God by following the Commandments, we show our love for God.

Concepts of Faith

How should we show our love for God?
We should show our love for God by choosing to follow the Commandments that He gave us.

Activity

Work together with your child on a small project or task. Have your child help you make a cake, wash the car, set the table, make a bed, etc. Point out the steps or directions you follow to do this project or task the correct way.

Lesson 5 *Directions:* Match the action to the place.

We show our love for God in different ways.

62

NOTE TO PARENTS

Lesson 5: Love Others as God Loves You

The story for this lesson is an adaptation of Luke 10: 30–37. We are made in the image of God to do what God does. God loves us, God loves everyone. That means that, because God loves us and everyone, we should love ourselves and everyone else. First we should love God, then we should love ourselves, and then we should love others as God loves us. When we love others, we make ourselves happy because we are acting as God made us to act.

Concepts of Faith

Who does God love?
God loves everyone.

Who are we to love?
We are to love God, ourselves, and everyone else.

Activity

Give your child an extra hug. Say "I love you."

Lesson 5 *Directions:* Cut out the pictures. Put them in the correct order.

NOTE TO PARENTS

Lesson 5: Love Others as God Loves You

The story for this lesson is an adaptation of Luke 10: 30–37. We are made in the image of God to do what God does. God loves us, God loves everyone. That means that, because God loves us and everyone, we should love ourselves and everyone else. First we should love God, then we should love ourselves, and then we should love others as God loves us. When we love others, we make ourselves happy because we are acting as God made us to act.

Concepts of Faith

Who does God love?
God loves everyone.

Who are we to love?
We are to love God, ourselves, and everyone else.

Activity

Give your child an extra hug. Say "I love you."

Lesson 6 Directions: Circle the items we see in God's house.

The church is God's house on earth.

64

NOTE TO PARENTS

Lesson 6: God's House—The Church

From this lesson, the children should come to respect the items found in the church and come to know the correct behavior for church. God's house is a place of prayer and celebration. Mass is our most important prayer. At Mass, stories about God are read, and God gives us the gift of Himself at Communion. Sitting quietly and listening to the stories about God, saying prayers, singing the songs, and showing respect for the things found in God's house can be gifts of love offered to God. We should be careful with the books and other things we see in church. We should remember that God is in church with us in a very special way.

Concepts of Faith

What is God's house on earth called?
God's house on earth is called the church.

Activity

Visit your parish church when there are no services. Let your child walk around the church looking at the statues, stained glass windows, etc.

Lesson 6 *Directions:* Cut out the children. Put them in the pew.

We sit quietly in church.

65

NOTE TO PARENTS

Lesson 6: God's House—The Church

From this lesson, the children should come to respect the items found in the church and come to know the correct behavior for church. God's house is a place of prayer and celebration. Mass is our most important prayer. At Mass, stories about God are read, and God gives us the gift of Himself at Communion. Sitting quietly and listening to the stories about God, saying prayers, singing the songs, and showing respect for the things found in God's house can be gifts of love offered to God. We should be careful with the books and other things we see in church. We should remember that God is in church with us in a very special way.

Concepts of Faith

What is God's house on earth called?
God's house on earth is called the church.

Activity

Visit your parish church when there are no services. Let your child walk around the church looking at the statues, stained glass windows, etc.

Lesson 7 *Directions:* Circle the tree that is different.

God said, "Do not eat from the tree of good and bad."

NOTE TO PARENTS

Lesson 7: Wrong Choices—Sin

The story for this lesson is an adaptation of Genesis 3: 1-24. Even though most of the children are not of the age of reason and thus technically cannot sin, it is important to establish a sense of right and wrong. Along with this awareness of morality should come a sense of sorrow and a need for forgiveness when a wrong is committed. When we choose to do something we know is wrong, we are not clear images of God. We have displeased God. Sin is the opposite of love.

Concepts of Faith

How do we sin?
We sin by choosing to do something we know is wrong. We disobey God. We do not love Him as we should.

What happens when we sin?
When we sin, we hurt ourselves, we hurt others, and we displease God.

Activity

Let your child choose an appropriate snack to make as a surprise for the rest of the family.

Lesson 7 *Directions:* Color the picture.

Adam and Eve disobeyed God.

NOTE TO PARENTS

Lesson 7: Wrong Choices—Sin

The story for this lesson is an adaptation of Genesis 3: 1–24. Even though most of the children are not of the age of reason and thus technically cannot sin, it is important to establish a sense of right and wrong. Along with this awareness of morality should come a sense of sorrow and a need for forgiveness when a wrong is committed. When we choose to do something we know is wrong, we are not clear images of God. We have displeased God. Sin is the opposite of love.

Concepts of Faith

How do we sin?
We sin by choosing to do something we know is wrong. We disobey God. We do not love Him as we should.

What happens when we sin?
When we sin, we hurt ourselves, we hurt others, and we displease God.

Activity

Let your child choose an appropriate snack to make as a surprise for the rest of the family.

Lesson 8 *Directions:* Connect the lines and color the picture.

God said, "This is my Son. He has pleased Me."

NOTE TO PARENTS

Lesson 8: God's Family—Baptism

The story for this lesson is an adaptation of Matt. 3: 13-17. Baptism is the beginning and the foundation of our union with God. Through the sacrament of baptism, we receive the gift of grace. Grace is God's own life. Grace makes it possible for us to act as images of God and makes us members of God's family. Therefore, grace helps us get to heaven.

Concepts of Faith

Who are members of God's family?
All baptized people are members of God's family.

What is grace?
Grace is a share in God's own life.

Activity

Together look at pictures from your child's baptism. Discuss that special day.

Lesson 8 *Directions:* Color the picture.

At baptism we become members of God's family.

69

NOTE TO PARENTS

Lesson 8: God's Family—Baptism

The story for this lesson is an adaptation of Matt. 3: 13–17. Baptism is the beginning and the foundation of our union with God. Through the sacrament of baptism, we receive the gift of grace. Grace is God's own life. Grace makes it possible for us to act as images of God and makes us members of God's family. Therefore, grace helps us get to heaven.

Concepts of Faith

Who are members of God's family?
All baptized people are members of God's family.

What is grace?
Grace is a share in God's own life.

Activity

Together look at pictures from your child's baptism. Discuss that special day.

Lesson 9   *Directions:* Draw a happy or sad face.

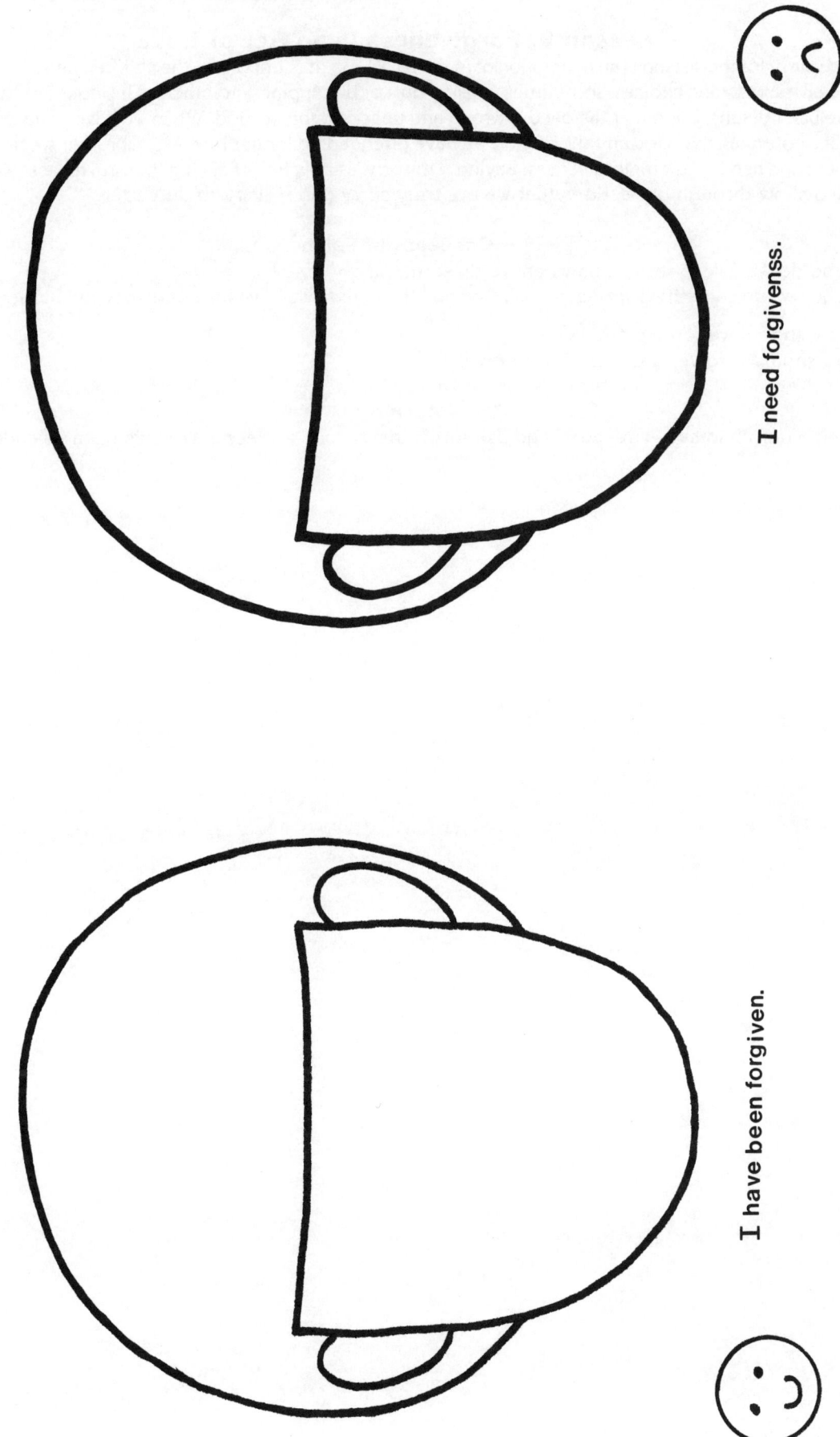

I need forgivenss.

I have been forgiven.

Forgive others as God forgives you.

NOTE TO PARENTS

Lesson 9: Forgiveness Is an Act of Love

The story for this lesson is an adaptation of Matt. 18: 21-35. It is important the children understand that we all make wrong choices, sometimes causing hurt or unhappiness to others. This does not mean we are bad persons, but rather the deed is wrong and unacceptable to God. When we have done wrong, it does not mean that God and the person we have offended no longer love us, but rather we have hurt them and need to ask for forgiveness. Saying "I'm sorry" is only half of asking for forgiveness. We must also show through our actions that we are truly sorry and will try to do better.

Concepts of Faith

Who do we ask to forgive us when we do something wrong?
When we do something wrong, we ask God and the person we have hurt or disobeyed to forgive us.

How should we forgive others?
We should forgive others as God forgives us.

Activity

Help your child say "I'm sorry" and ask forgiveness from someone who has been offended.

Lesson 9 *Directions:* Connect the lines and color the picture.

Forgiveness is an act of love.

NOTE TO PARENTS

Lesson 9: Forgiveness Is an Act of Love

The story for this lesson is an adaptation of Matt. 18: 21-35. It is important the children understand that we all make wrong choices, sometimes causing hurt or unhappiness to others. This does not mean we are bad persons, but rather the deed is wrong and unacceptable to God. When we have done wrong, it does not mean that God and the person we have offended no longer love us, but rather we have hurt them and need to ask for forgiveness. Saying "I'm sorry" is only half of asking for forgiveness. We must also show through our actions that we are truly sorry and will try to do better.

Concepts of Faith

Who do we ask to forgive us when we do something wrong?
When we do something wrong, we ask God and the person we have hurt or disobeyed to forgive us.

How should we forgive others?
We should forgive others as God forgives us.

Activity

Help your child say "I'm sorry" and ask forgiveness from someone who has been offended.

Lesson 10 Our Father Booklet

Our Father who art in heaven,

God, our Father, is in heaven.

hallowed be Thy name.

God's name is holy.

72

NOTE TO PARENTS

Lesson 10: Prayer

The story for this lesson is an adaptation of Luke 18: 9–14. The "Our Father" is introduced in this lesson. Jesus prayed often and taught others how to pray. Jesus wants us to follow His example and pray often to our Father in heaven. God hears all our prayers even when we do not say the words out loud. Sometimes we do not get what we pray for because God knows what is best for us.

Concepts of Faith

What is prayer?
Prayer is talking to God quietly or out loud, alone or with others. We can say "thank you," ask for help, say "I'm sorry," and sing God's praises.

Activity

Review the "Our Father" with your child.

Lesson 10 Our Father Booklet

and forgive us our trespasses as we forgive those who trespass against us,

Forgive us for our sins and help us forgive others.

and lead us not into temptation,
but deliver us from evil. Amen.

Help us to make good choices
and keep us safe in your love.

Lesson 11 *Directions:* Connect the dots and color the picture.

The woman found something much better than water.

75

NOTE TO PARENTS

Lesson 11: Jesus Is God the Son

The story for this lesson is an adaptation of John 4: 4–30. Jesus is God the Son, the second Person of the Blessed Trinity. Jesus is the One Whose coming was foretold in the Scriptures. He came down from heaven to save us from our sins, that is, to redeem us. Thus, He shows us who we are and makes it possible for us to live as images of God now and to be happy forever with God in heaven.

Concepts of Faith

Who is Jesus?
Jesus is God the Son.

Activity

Show your child your family bible or a bible you use.

Lesson 11 *Directions:* Color the dotted areas.

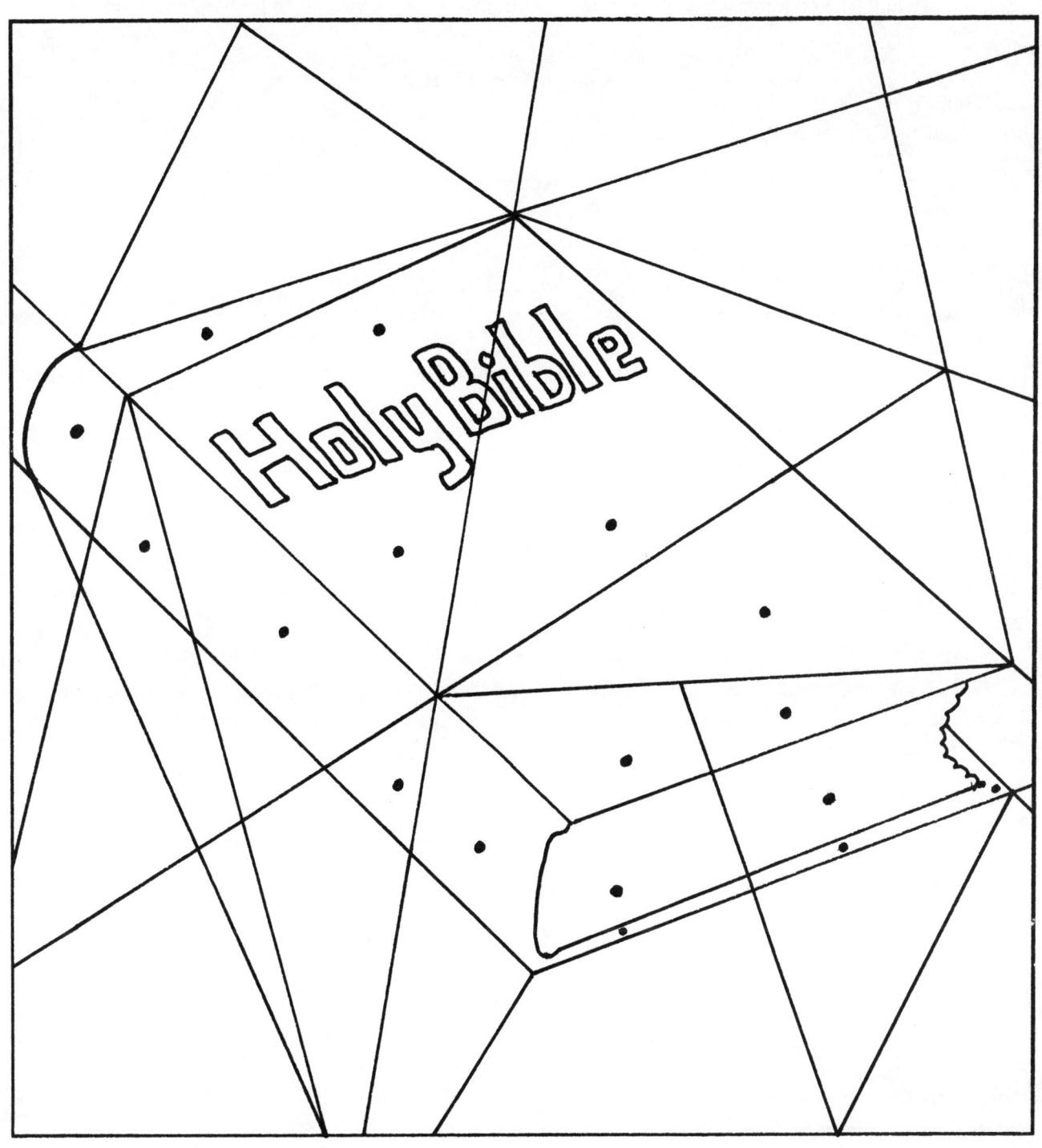

The bible is a book about God and Jesus' life on earth.

NOTE TO PARENTS

Lesson 11: Jesus Is God the Son

The story for this lesson is an adaptation of John 4: 4–30. Jesus is God the Son, the second Person of the Blessed Trinity. Jesus is the One Whose coming was foretold in the Scriptures. He came down from heaven to save us from our sins, that is, to redeem us. Thus, He shows us who we are and makes it possible for us to live as images of God now and to be happy forever with God in heaven.

Concepts of Faith

Who is Jesus?
Jesus is God the Son.

Activity

Show your child your family bible or a bible you use.

Lesson 12   Directions: Circle the miracles.

Jesus can do miracles because He is God the Son.

77

NOTE TO PARENTS

Lesson 12: Miracles of Jesus

The story for this lesson is an adaptation of John 6: 1–15. The miracles that Jesus performed were not done by magic tricks. Jesus really did heal the sick, change water into wine, multiply the loaves and fishes. He could perform miracles because He is God the Son. The miracles Jesus worked helped people believe in what He said. As images of God, we can help others believe in and follow Jesus.

Concepts of Faith

Who is Jesus?
Jesus is God the Son.

Activity

You and your child may work together to do something nice for another member of your family. Talk about how Jesus helped others.

Lesson 12 *Directions:* Connect the dots and color the picture.

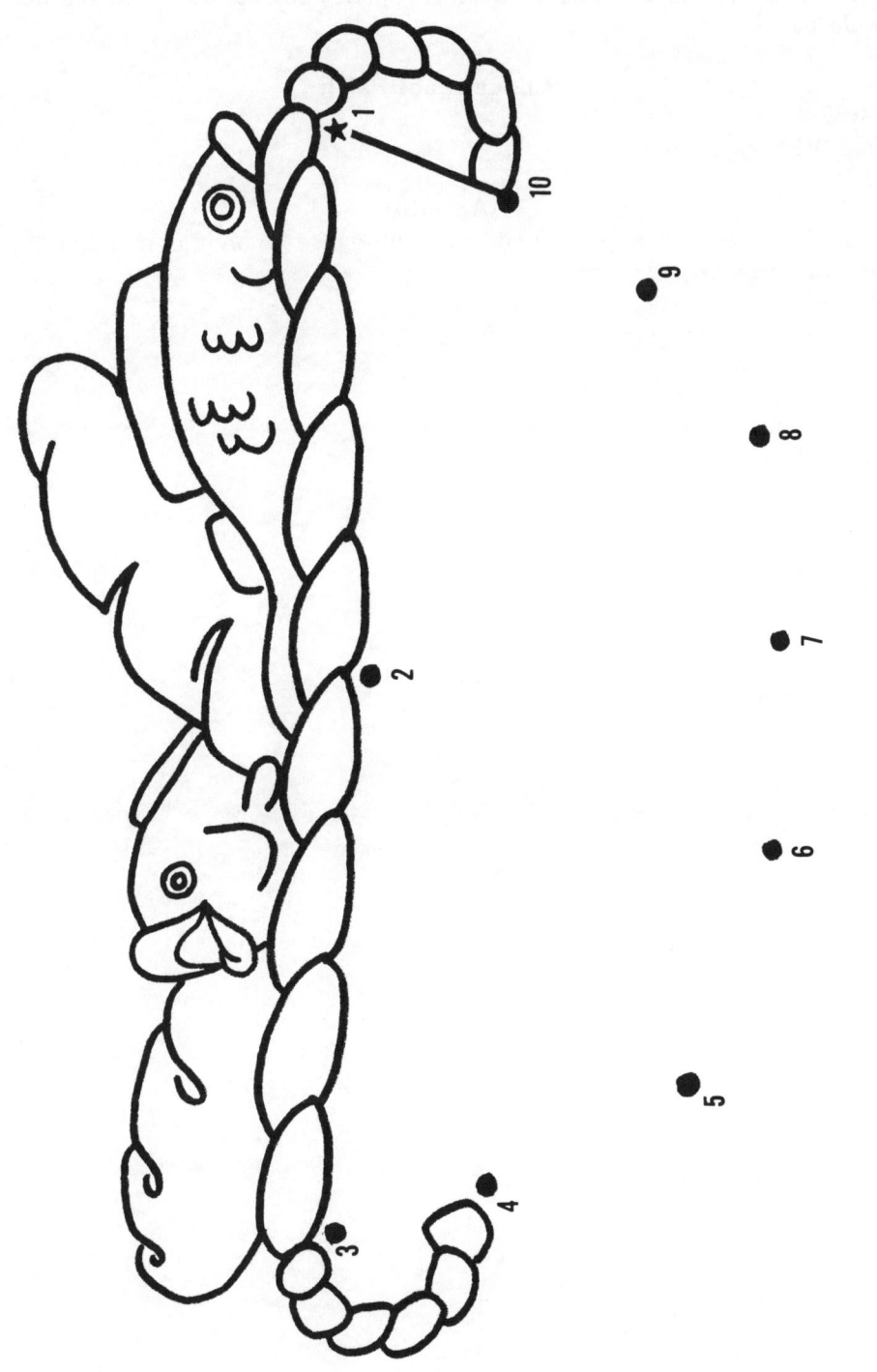

Jesus worked a miracle.

78

NOTE TO PARENTS

Lesson 12: Miracles of Jesus

The story for this lesson is an adaptation of John 6: 1–15. The miracles that Jesus performed were not done by magic tricks. Jesus really did heal the sick, change water into wine, multiply the loaves and fishes. He could perform miracles because He is God the Son. The miracles Jesus worked helped people believe in what He said. As images of God, we can help others believe in and follow Jesus.

Concepts of Faith

Who is Jesus?
Jesus is God the Son.

Activity

You and your child may work together to do something nice for another member of your family. Talk about how Jesus helped others.

Lesson 13 *Directions:* Find and color the hidden fish.

Jesus asked the fishermen to follow Him.

NOTE TO PARENTS

Lesson 13: Jesus Says, "Come Follow Me"

The story for this lesson is an adaptation of Matt. 4: 18–22. Jesus extended the invitation to follow Him repeatedly throughout His life on earth. He extended the invitation to follow Him (to do as He did) to apostles. They answered Jesus' call and chose to follow Him and lead others to Him. Jesus asks all people to follow Him. We follow Jesus by being the best image of God we can be.

Concepts of Faith

Who were the apostles?
The apostles were special friends of Jesus who answered His call and chose to follow Him and teach others about Him.

Activity

Play "follow the leader" with your child.

Lesson 13 *Directions:* Follow the footprints to heaven.

Jesus said, "Come follow Me."

NOTE TO PARENTS

Lesson 13: Jesus Says, "Come Follow Me"

The story for this lesson is an adaptation of Matt. 4: 18–22. Jesus extended the invitation to follow Him repeatedly throughout His life on earth. He extended the invitation to follow Him (to do as He did) to apostles. They answered Jesus' call and chose to follow Him and lead others to Him. Jesus asks all people to follow Him. We follow Jesus by being the best image of God we can be.

Concepts of Faith

Who were the apostles?
The apostles were special friends of Jesus who answered His call and chose to follow Him and teach others about Him.

Activity

Play "follow the leader" with your child.

Lesson 14 *Directions:* Connect the dots and color the picture.

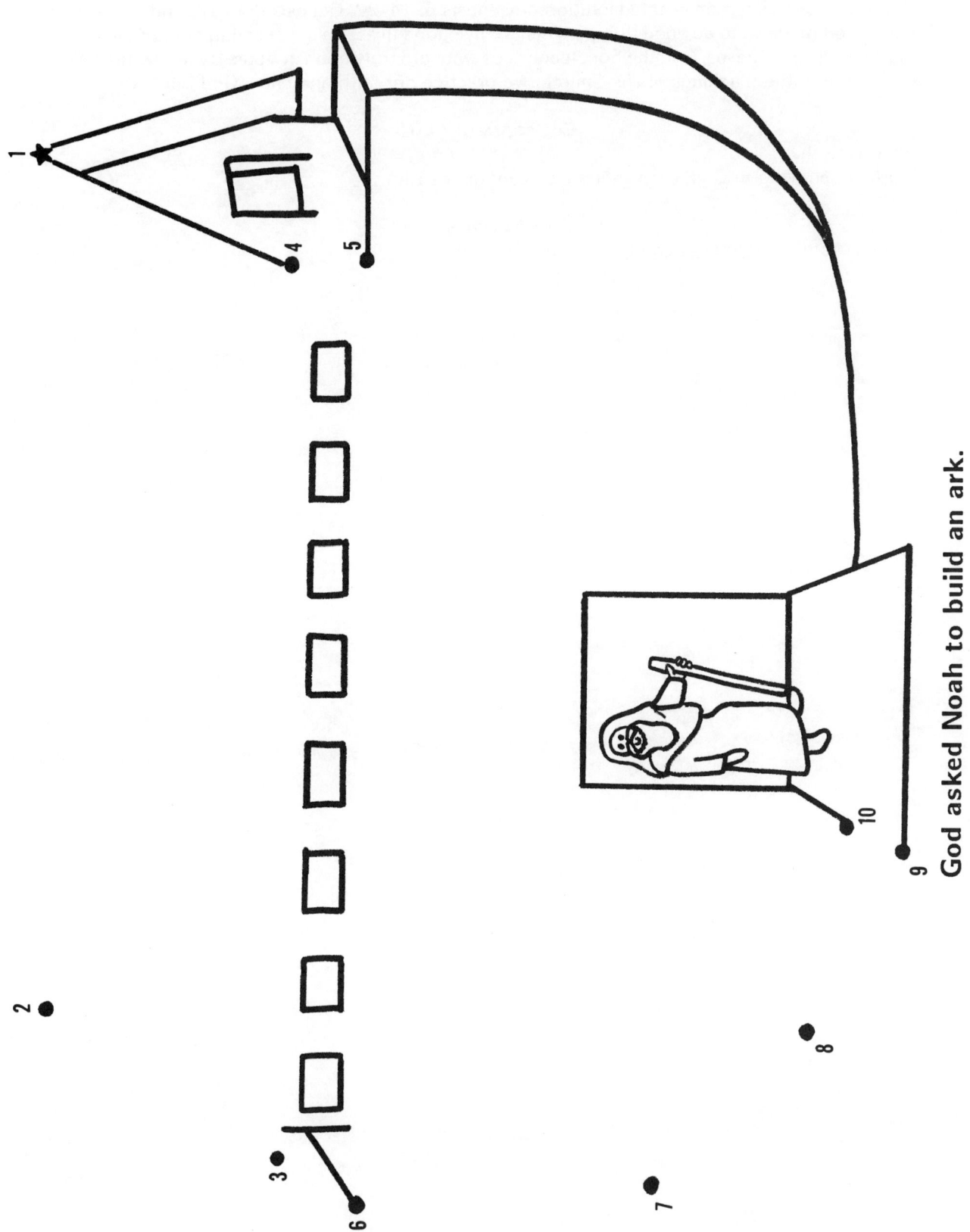

God asked Noah to build an ark.

NOTE TO PARENTS

Lesson 14: Faith and Trust

The story for this lesson is an adaptation of Genesis 6: 14–22, Genesis 8: 6–12, and Genesis 9: 8–17. God made us to do good things. When we live good lives, we are showing our faith and saying "yes" to God. Jesus, God the Son, teaches us what are truly good actions. By following Jesus' example and the teachings of His Church, we practice our faith and show God our love.

Concepts of Faith

What is faith?
Faith is believing in God, even though we cannot see Him.

Activity

Read a bible story to your child.

Lesson 14   *Directions:* Match the animals that are the same.

Noah led two of every animal to the ark.

NOTE TO PARENTS

Lesson 14: Faith and Trust

The story for this lesson is an adaptation of Genesis 6: 14–22, Genesis 8: 6–12, and Genesis 9: 8–17. God made us to do good things. When we live good lives, we are showing our faith and saying "yes" to God. Jesus, God the Son, teaches us what are truly good actions. By following Jesus' example and the teachings of His Church, we practice our faith and show God our love.

Concepts of Faith

What is faith?
Faith is believing in God, even though we cannot see Him.

Activity

Read a bible story to your child.

Lesson 15 *Directions:* Color the picture.

Jesus said, "Little girl get up."

NOTE TO PARENTS

Lesson 15: After Death Is Life

The story for this lesson is an adaptation of Mark 5: 21–24 and Mark 5: 35–43. When someone dies, that person's life does not end; it changes. When people die, they begin new lives with God in heaven, if they have followed Jesus' example. We are still images of God even after we have died. We pray for all those who have died so they may receive new life with God in heaven.

Concepts of Faith

Is dying the end of our lives?
No, if we have lived as images of God then it is the beginning of new life with God in heaven.

Activity

Tell your child about a relative or friend who has died. Say a prayer with your child for that person.

Lesson 15   *Directions:* Cut out the wings. Put them on the butterfly.

A butterfly is a sign of new life.

84

NOTE TO PARENTS

Lesson 15: After Death Is Life

The story for this lesson is an adaptation of Mark 5: 21–24 and Mark 5: 35–43. When someone dies, that person's life does not end; it changes. When people die, they begin new lives with God in heaven, if they have followed Jesus' example. We are still images of God even after we have died. We pray for all those who have died so they may receive new life with God in heaven.

Concepts of Faith

Is dying the end of our lives?
No, if we have lived as images of God then it is the beginning of new life with God in heaven.

Activity

Tell your child about a relative or friend who has died. Say a prayer with your child for that person.

Lesson 16   *Directions:* Circle the good actions.

Our good actions show that God is most important in our lives.

85

NOTE TO PARENTS

Lesson 16: God Should Come First in Our Lives

The story for this lesson is an adaptation of Matt. 7: 24–29. When we live our lives showing that we are images of God in all we "think, and say, and do," then we show that God comes first for us. It may not always be easy to do what is right, but when we obey and think of others before ourselves, we are living as Jesus taught and showing that God is most important in our lives. The material things we have—toys, jewelry, houses, money, etc.—are good and are for our use, but they are not the most important part of life. God should be Number 1 in our lives.

Concepts of Faith

Who is most important in our lives?
God is most important in our lives.

How do we show God is most important?
We show that God is most important by acting as images of God in all we "think, and say, and do."

Activity

Have your child gather some outgrown toys or clothes to give to the needy.

Lesson 16   *Directions:* Color the picture.

**The wise man built his house on the rock.
We should build our lives with God.**

NOTE TO PARENTS

Lesson 16: God Should Come First in Our Lives

The story for this lesson is an adaptation of Matt. 7: 24–29. When we live our lives showing that we are images of God in all we "think, and say, and do," then we show that God comes first for us. It may not always be easy to do what is right, but when we obey and think of others before ourselves, we are living as Jesus taught and showing that God is most important in our lives. The material things we have—toys, jewelry, houses, money, etc.—are good and are for our use, but they are not the most important part of life. God should be Number 1 in our lives.

Concepts of Faith

Who is most important in our lives?
God is most important in our lives.

How do we show God is most important?
We show that God is most important by acting as images of God in all we "think, and say, and do."

Activity

Have your child gather some outgrown toys or clothes to give to the needy.

Lesson 17   *Directions:* Help the shepherd find his lost sheep.

The good shepherd took care of his sheep.

NOTE TO PARENTS

Lesson 17: God Cares for Us and All He Has Made

The story for this lesson is an adaptation of Matt. 18: 10–14 and John 10: 11–15. God is the source of all we have and all we need. He loves us. He wants to share His life with us now and He wants us to be with Him someday in heaven. God has told us, shown us, and given us all that we need to be the best images of God we can be. Jesus told us that God takes care of all that He has made. We know God loves and takes care of us.

Concepts of Faith

Who takes care of us always?
God takes care of us always.

Who did God give to each one of us to help and guide us?
God gave each one of us a guardian angel to help and guide us.

Activity

Review the "Guardian Angel" prayer with your child: **Angel of God, my guardian dear, to whom God's love commits me here, ever this day be at my side, to light and guard, to rule and guide. Amen.**

Lesson 17   *Directions:* Color the dotted areas.

**Jesus is our good shepherd.
He loves and takes care of us.**

NOTE TO PARENTS

Lesson 17: God Cares for Us and All He Has Made

The story for this lesson is an adaptation of Matt. 18: 10–14 and John 10: 11–15. God is the source of all we have and all we need. He loves us. He wants to share His life with us now and He wants us to be with Him someday in heaven. God has told us, shown us, and given us all that we need to be the best images of God we can be. Jesus told us that God takes care of all that He has made. We know God loves and takes care of us.

Concepts of Faith

Who takes care of us always?
God takes care of us always.

Who did God give to each one of us to help and guide us?
God gave each one of us a guardian angel to help and guide us.

Activity

Review the "Guardian Angel" prayer with your child: **Angel of God, my guardian dear, to whom God's love commits me here, ever this day be at my side, to light and guard, to rule and guide. Amen.**

Thanksgiving   *Directions:* Cut out the food. Put the food on the plate.

Thank you, God, for all You have given us.

NOTE TO PARENTS

Lesson 19: Thanksgiving

The story for this lesson is an adaptation of Luke 17: 11–19. Thanksgiving is not just a time for a big meal with family and friends. It is a time for all God's family to join together to say "thank you" and to give praise to our loving Father who made all things. Through our prayers, we thank God for all He has given us. We also show God we are thankful by taking care of what He has given us.

Activity

Recite the "Blessing before Meals" with your child: **Bless us, O Lord, and these Thy gifts which we are about to receive from Thy bounty, through Christ, our Lord. Amen.**

Advent (1)   *Directions:* Circle the items that remind us of Jesus' birthday.

During advent we prepare our hearts and homes for Jesus' birthday.

NOTE TO PARENTS

Lesson 20: Advent 1—Preparing Our Hearts and Homes

As we wait for the celebration of Jesus' birthday, Christmas, we prepare our homes, and more importantly, our hearts. During the waiting period, Advent, there are many ways in which we can show our love for God and others. It is important we share the true meaning of Christmas, that is, love, in our daily lives throughout the entire year and not just during this season.

Concepts of Faith

Who is Jesus?
Jesus is God the Son.

When do we celebrate Jesus' birthday?
We celebrate Jesus' birthday on Christmas.

Activity

Use an Advent wreath with your family to count the weeks until Christmas.

Advent (1)

Directions: Cut out the candles. Glue them on the wreath.

Advent is a time of waiting for Jesus' birthday.

NOTE TO PARENTS

Lesson 20: Advent 1—Preparing Our Hearts and Homes

As we wait for the celebration of Jesus' birthday, Christmas, we prepare our homes, and more importantly, our hearts. During the waiting period, Advent, there are many ways in which we can show our love for God and others. It is important we share the true meaning of Christmas, that is, love, in our daily lives throughout the entire year and not just during this season.

Concepts of Faith

Who is Jesus?
Jesus is God the Son.

When do we celebrate Jesus' birthday?
We celebrate Jesus' birthday on Christmas.

Activity

Use an Advent wreath with your family to count the weeks until Christmas.

Advent (2)

Directions: Circle the things Mary would need for baby Jesus.

Mary loved and cared for Jesus like our mothers take care of us.

NOTE TO PARENTS

Lesson 21: Advent 2—Mary Said "Yes" to God

The story for this lesson is an adaptation of Luke 1: 26–45. Mary willingly chose to do what God asked her to do. Mary is an example for all people. She showed her love for God in all she "thought, and said, and did." We should follow her example. We ask Mary to pray for all of us so we will be more like her and her Son, Jesus.

Concepts of Faith

Who is Mary?
Mary is the Mother of God.

Activity

Recite the "Hail Mary" with your child: **Hail Mary, full of grace, the Lord is with thee. Blessed art thou among women and blessed is the fruit of thy womb, Jesus. Holy Mary, Mother of God, pray for us sinners now, and at the hour of our death. Amen.**

Advent (2)

Directions: Cut out baby Jesus. Lay Him in Mary's arms.

Mary is Jesus' mother.

93

NOTE TO PARENTS

Lesson 21: Advent 2—Mary Said "Yes" to God

The story for this lesson is an adaptation of Luke 1: 26–45. Mary willingly chose to do what God asked her to do. Mary is an example for all people. She showed her love for God in all she "thought, and said, and did." We should follow her example. We ask Mary to pray for all of us so we will be more like her and her Son, Jesus.

Concepts of Faith

Who is Mary?
Mary is the Mother of God.

Activity

Recite the "Hail Mary" with your child: **Hail Mary, full of grace, the Lord is with thee. Blessed art thou among women and blessed is the fruit of thy womb, Jesus. Holy Mary, Mother of God, pray for us sinners now, and at the hour of our death. Amen.**

Advent (3)   *Directions:* Connect the dots and color the picture.

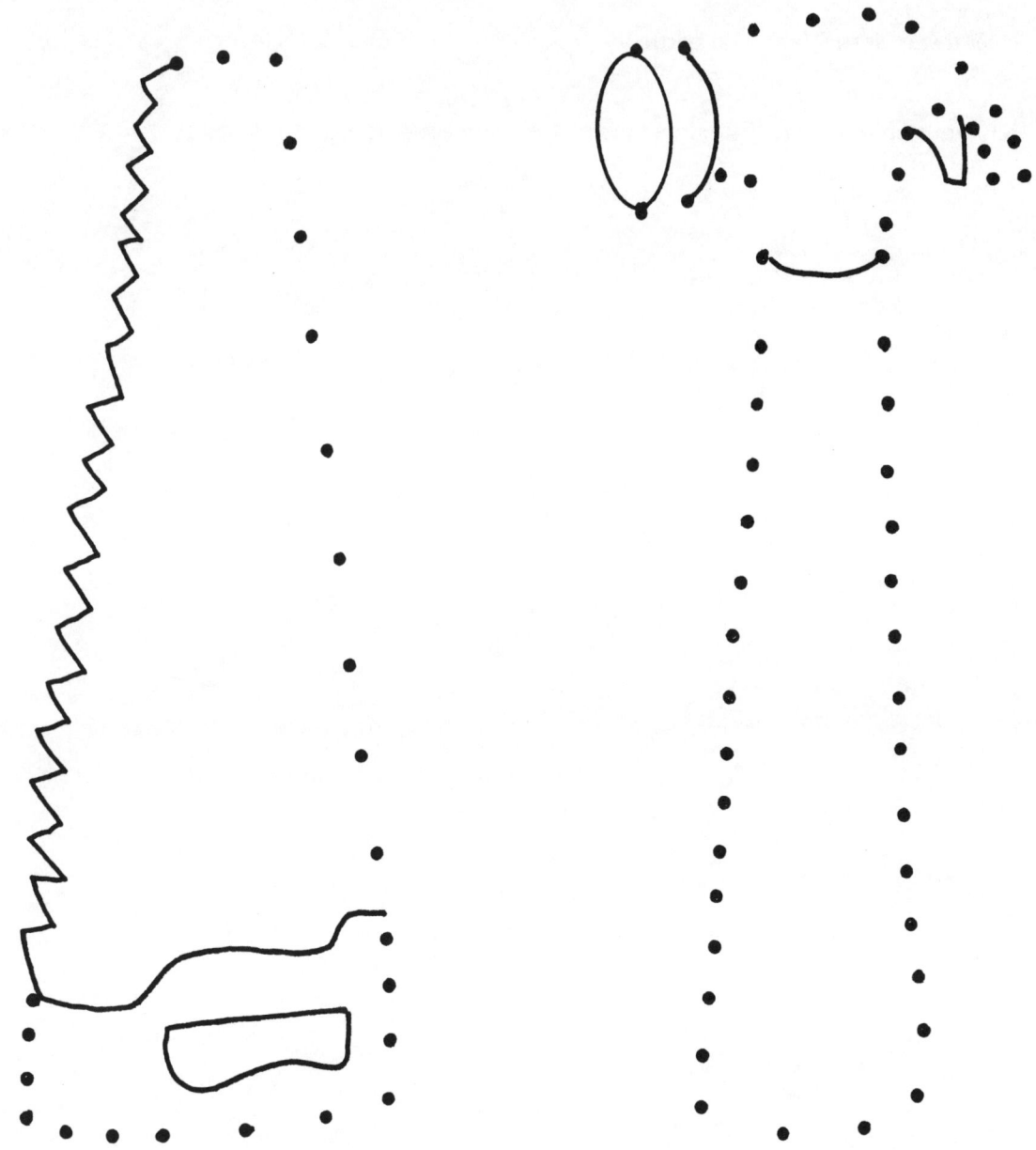

**Joseph was a carpenter.
He made things out of wood.**

NOTE TO PARENTS

Lesson 22: Advent 3—Joseph, Jesus' Father on Earth

The story for this lesson is an adaptation of Matt. 1: 18–25 and Luke 2: 1–7. Joseph received special graces from God to be the head of the Holy Family. He was chosen by God to be Jesus' foster father and Mary's husband. Like Jesus and Mary, Joseph chose to obey the will of God in all things. He cared for Jesus and Mary out of love for them and for God.

Concepts of Faith

Who was Joseph?
Joseph was Jesus' father on earth.

Activity

Help your child make a Christmas present for someone as a gift of love.

Advent (3)

Directions: Help Joseph and Mary find the stable.

Joseph and Mary traveled to Bethlehem.

NOTE TO PARENTS

Lesson 22: Advent 3—Joseph, Jesus' Father on Earth

The story for this lesson is an adaptation of Matt. 1: 18–25 and Luke 2: 1–7. Joseph received special graces from God to be the head of the Holy Family. He was chosen by God to be Jesus' foster father and Mary's husband. Like Jesus and Mary, Joseph chose to obey the will of God in all things. He cared for Jesus and Mary out of love for them and for God.

Concepts of Faith

Who was Joseph?
Joseph was Jesus' father on earth.

Activity

Help your child make a Christmas present for someone as a gift of love.

Advent (4)

Directions: Connect the dots and color the picture.

Jesus' bed was called a manger.

NOTE TO PARENTS

Lesson 23: Advent 4—Christmas Is Jesus' Birthday

The story for this lesson is an adaptation of Luke 2: 1–18. Jesus teaches us that life is truly a celebration of love to be offered to God. On His birthday, we renew our commitment to a life of love and pray that our hearts be filled with the peace and love of the Christ Child. Christmas is a worldwide celebration of love; the love God has for us and the love we have for God and others.

Concepts of Faith

What is Christmas?
Christmas is Jesus' birthday.

Activity

Help your child set up a Nativity scene in anticipation of Christmas.

Advent (4) *Directions:* Cut out baby Jesus. Lay Him in the manger.

Mary laid baby Jesus in the manger.

NOTE TO PARENTS

Lesson 23: Advent 4—Christmas Is Jesus' Birthday

The story for this lesson is an adaptation of Luke 2: 1–18. Jesus teaches us that life is truly a celebration of love to be offered to God. On His birthday, we renew our commitment to a life of love and pray that our hearts be filled with the peace and love of the Christ Child. Christmas is a worldwide celebration of love; the love God has for us and the love we have for God and others.

Concepts of Faith

What is Christmas?
Christmas is Jesus' birthday.

Activity

Help your child set up a Nativity scene in anticipation of Christmas.

Ash Wednesday   *Directions:* Circle the things that remind us Easter is near.

Lent is a time for preparing ourselves for the joy and new life of Easter.

NOTE TO PARENTS

Lesson 24: Lent

During Lent we make sacrifices to offer to God. We "do without" things such as a favorite television show or treats. We give up something to show God we love Him, and that He is most important to us. Jesus gave up His life for us because He loves us.

Concepts of Faith

What is Lent?
Lent is a time for preparing ourselves for the joy and new life of Easter.

Activity

As a family decide to do something during Lent that shows God you love Him.

Palm Sunday   *Directions:* Connect the dots and color the picture.

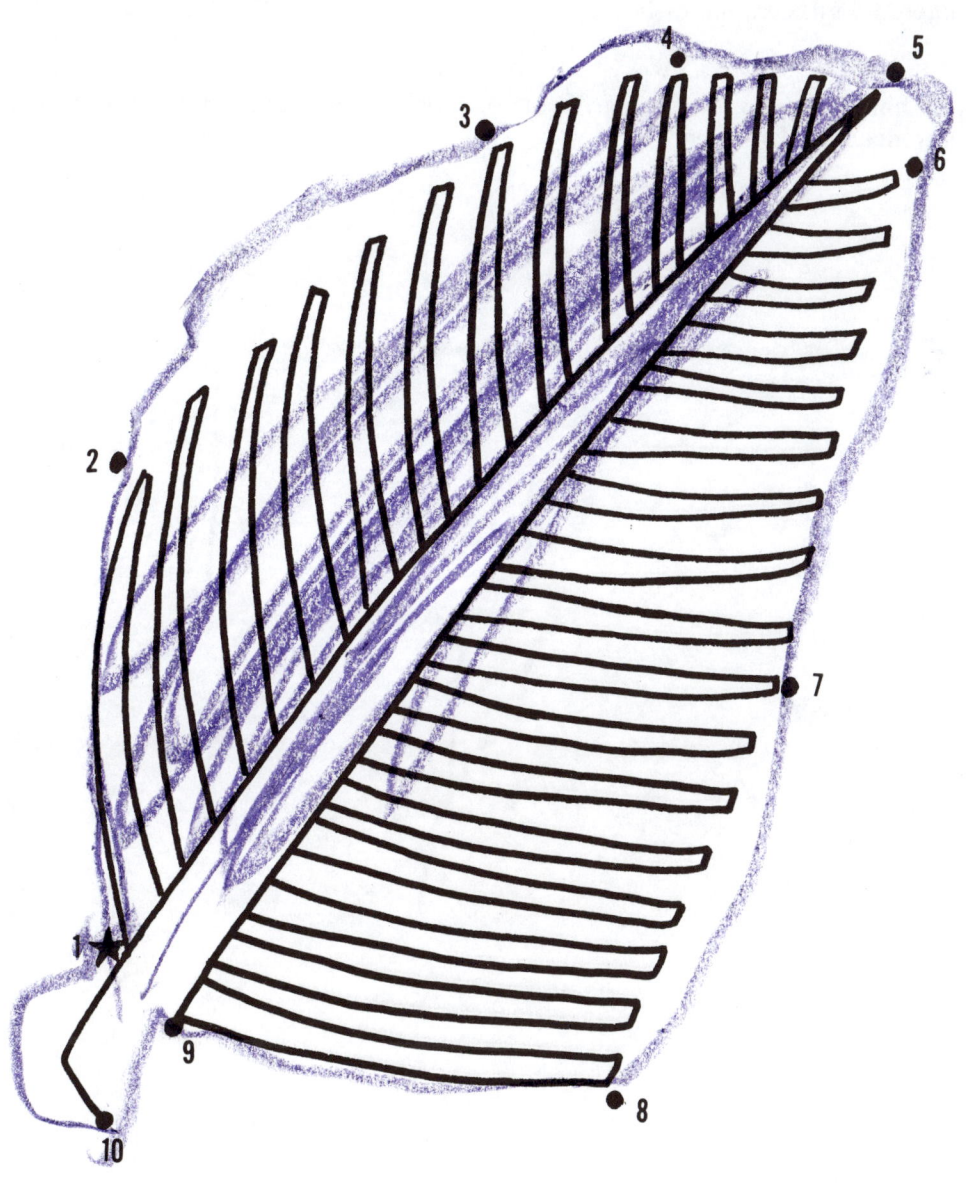

The people shouted "Hosanna" and laid palm branches on the road.

NOTE TO PARENTS

Lesson 26: Palm Sunday

Palm Sunday is the beginning of Holy Week. On the first Palm Sunday, Jesus entered Jerusalem amid the cheers and the praises of the people, a definite contrast to what would happen to Him at the end of this Holy Week.

Concepts of Faith

What happened on Palm Sunday?
Jesus entered Jerusalem amid shouts of praise.

Activity

Show your child the palm branches given out at church. Tell your child the story of Jesus' triumphant entrance into Jerusalem.

Holy Week *Directions:* Trace the letters.

THIS IS MY BODY

NOTE TO PARENTS

Lesson 27: Holy Week

Holy Week includes Palm Sunday, the day people sang Hosanna to Jesus; Holy Thursday, the day of the Last Supper; Good Friday, the day Jesus died; and Holy Saturday, the day Jesus' body lay in the tomb.

Concepts of Faith

What happened on Holy Thursday?
On Holy Thursday Jesus and the apostles shared the Last Supper, the first Mass.

What happened on Good Friday?
On Good Friday Jesus died on the cross.

Activity

Show your child a picture of the Last Supper and a picture of Jesus on the Cross.

Easter *Directions:* Connect the dots and color the picture.

Alleluia! He is risen.

NOTE TO PARENTS

Lesson 28: Easter Sunday

Easter is the celebration of new life. At this time we remember Jesus' triumph over death, His resurrection. Easter is the most joyous feast of the Church, celebrating the "new life" we receive from Jesus. We want to live with Jesus now, and someday we hope to be with Him in heaven.

Concepts of Faith

What happened on Easter Sunday?
On Easter Sunday Jesus rose from the dead.

Activity

Go on a spring walk with your child. Look for signs of new life.

Easter   *Directions:* Color the dotted areas.

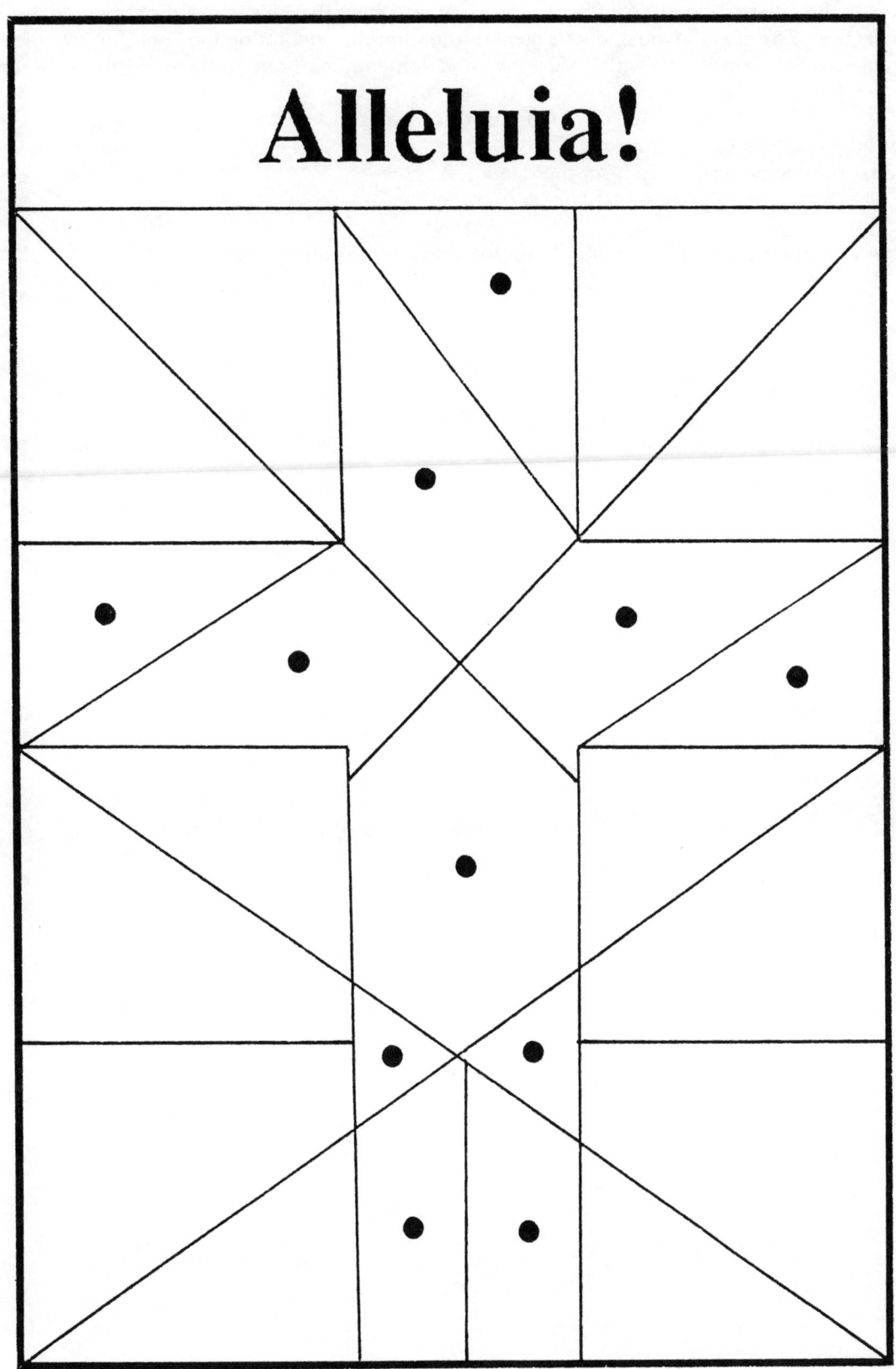

Alleluia! He is risen.

NOTE TO PARENTS

Lesson 28: Easter Sunday

Easter is the celebration of new life. At this time we remember Jesus' triumph over death, His resurrection. Easter is the most joyous feast of the Church, celebrating the "new life" we receive from Jesus. We want to live with Jesus now, and someday we hope to be with Him in heaven.

Concepts of Faith

What happened on Easter Sunday?
On Easter Sunday Jesus rose from the dead.

Activity

Go on a spring walk with your child. Look for signs of new life.